- THE BOOK OF -
Black Royalty

BY: IBRAHIM KONTEH & KWAME GAYLE
ILLUSTRATED BY: ADA EZENWA-AUTREY

"Dedicated to Zion, Sierra and all the children of Mother Earth."

CONTENTS

	PAGE
CLEOPATRA VII	1
RAMSES THE GREAT	3
MAKEDA: QUEEN OF SHEBA	5
MANSA MUSA	7
NZINGA OF NDONGO AND MATAMBA	9
HANNIBAL OF CARTHAGE	11
RANAVALONA I	13
SHAKA ZULU	15
GLOSSARY	17

ACKNOWLEDGEMENT

Ibrahim - I would like to thank a few people that have helped us in the process of bringing this book to life.

I was first inspired by the words of reggae artist, **Jamar "*Chronixx*" McNaughton**, "*Tell me why every time we hear 'bout Africa, a shackles and chains... Africa exist long before the Middle Passage*", and dub poet, **Allan Hope** - better known as ***Mutabaruka*** - when he said, "*Slavery is not Africa's history. Slavery interrupted Africa's history.*"

Kimberly Boswell for her work in editing the script.

Russell McGibbon for digital contents and graphic edits.

Judanne Lennox and **Carole Beckford**.

Finally, my parents, **Rose Marie Broadbell** and **Winston Broadbell**, for laying the foundation with books and lessons of black empowerment.

Kwame – I would like to thank my parents, **Edwin** and **Nellie Gayle**, for literally bestowing me with my powerful name and setting me on a journey of empowerment and affirmation. **My schools in Jamaica** that fostered my sense of pride, worth and humility. **Macalester College** for inspiring me to take my place in the world. Lastly, to **my students** around the world, for showing me that education is truly my passion.

PREFACE

Two bright minds and a literature project. The spark of this book was lit in Mrs. Alicia Morgan-Bromfield's class at *Munro College*, a premier all-boys boarding school in Jamaica. Ibrahim and Kwame performed an *'Ode to Dr. Martin Luther King'* in front of the entire school for Black History Month celebrations and received raving reviews.

Though young, they both shared a deep interest in and passion for exploring, researching and celebrating black figures of excellence. This is why, years later, when Ibrahim despised the fact that his son, Zion wasn't being introduced to books that celebrated blackness, he knew who to collaborate with to bring this vision to reality.

The Book of Black Royalty contains stories we wish we were exposed to as children, rather than stumbling upon them in our adulthood. We hope that children (and adults) who read this book will be empowered to be the best versions of themselves. **YOU** are already royalty!

CLEOPATRA VII

Cleopatra was the princess of Egypt. When she was born, her father was the ruling **Pharaoh**. He made her travel with him so she picked up lots of information about art, history and how to rule a country. She was a smart and clever young woman and she was her father's favorite child. Cleopatra could speak seven languages and was very brilliant.

Cleopatra became queen at age 18, when her father died. She shared the throne with her younger brother. Her brother was only 12, but he did not want to share this position and forced Cleopatra out of the palace. At that time, Julius Caesar ruled the Roman Empire. Wrapped in a carpet and carried by a servant, Cleopatra snuck into his palace and met with Caesar while he was passing through her country. She won him over with her charm and beauty and he restored her power in Egypt. Caesar was so impressed with Cleopatra's kingdom that he used some of her ideas in Rome. They even had a son together.

Cleopatra built up the Egyptian economy and established trade with many neighboring nations. Although Cleopatra was ethnically Greek, she was loved by Egyptian people because she learned their language and identified herself as an Egyptian pharaoh. She did not need translators when talking to rulers from other kingdoms. Cleopatra's story was so spectacular that William Shakespeare, a very famous writer, made it into a popular modern play.

As one of the most powerful women in Egyptian history, Cleopatra is seen in many art pieces, books and television shows.

RAMSES THE GREAT

Ramses II was Egypt's greatest and most powerful **pharaoh**. He grew up in a huge palace by the edge of the River Nile. Ramses became the youngest captain of the army at only ten years old! He followed his father on many military operations and paid very close attention to everything his father did. When Ramses was 15, he lost his older brother, so he became the new crown prince. Ramses had a lot of responsibility at a very young age, but he was always ready for a challenge.

Ramses wanted to be a great leader like his father and be remembered forever. He was very clever and used crafty plans to defeat his enemies. Sea pirates tried to attack ships along the coast of Egypt, so he planned surprise attacks and beat them all. Even though he was a great military captain, he was also a peacemaker. Ramses created one of the first peace **treaties** in history between Egypt and Hatti who were at war. He built many temples, **monuments**, and cities in Egypt. He used his military training to secure the borders of Egypt so they were not attacked by other countries.

Nine kings that followed called themselves Ramses because they wanted to be just like him. He was very popular and the people of Egypt loved him. Ramses ruled for almost 70 years and led Egypt to its most powerful time. He will forever be known as Ramses the Great.

MAKEDA:
QUEEN OF SHEBA

Makeda, also known as the Queen of Sheba, is a famous woman in Jewish, Islamic and Ethiopian cultures. In Ethiopia, she was the mother of their first **emperor**, making her the highest mother of the royal **empire**. She is also known to have visited Solomon, the famous king of Israel. She heard of his fame and wanted to prove it for herself. While she was visiting him, Solomon fell in love with her. He thought she was extremely beautiful and full of potential so, he taught her about leadership and religion. They had a son together- Menelik - who became the first ruler of Ethiopia.

While Makeda was queen, Ethiopia was very powerful and famous. She took a small kingdom and made it one of the most respected in the world. She is believed to be a direct ancestor of Haile Selassie, a respected, Ethiopian ruler. In the Rastafarian religion, which was started on the island of Jamaica in the 1930s, Haile Selassie is **revered** as God in the flesh, the returned Messiah.

Today, you will find Makeda in many museums and she is talked about in churches, **synagogues** and **mosques**. Makeda is celebrated for her beauty, power and intelligence. She is a legend in Ethiopia and all over the world.

MANSA MUSA

Mansa Musa was the emperor of Mali for 25 years and the richest man in history! Mali was the largest producer of gold in the world and Mansa Musa owned most of it. If he were alive today, he would be worth 400 billion US dollars! Although he was **wealthy**, Mansa Musa was very kind. He gave presents and nuggets of gold to strangers because he believed that great riches should be shared. When people stopped in his country to do trade, he gave them food, clothing and shelter.

Mansa Musa also believed in the value of education and religion so he built the University of Sankore in Timbuktu and many large **mosques** and schools. He wanted to visit the holy city of Mecca, so he went on a **pilgrimage**. He traveled with thousands of people, wearing expensive silk clothing and giving away his gold along the way.

When he got to Mecca, he had given out so much that he needed to borrow some to return to his country. Because he was so generous, everybody was happy to lend him what he needed.

Many of the buildings Mansa Musa constructed are still standing today and his great **generosity** made Mali famous.

NZINGA
OF NDONGO AND MATAMBA

Queen Anna Nzinga Mbande was a powerful and intelligent ruler in Angola. It is said that her **umbilical cord** was caught around her neck when she was born. When everyone in her village heard this, they believed she would grow up to be proud and mighty. Nzinga's father was the king of Ndongo, a half of Angola at the time. She was her father's favorite child so he gave her access to all his plans and also took her to war. As a child, Nzinga saw Portuguese enemies taking **slaves** from her country. This made Nzinga sad and she decided to do everything she could to stop this from happening.

Her father made a treaty with the Portuguese to prevent them from taking his people as slaves but, after he died, they refused to follow his agreement. Her brother became the new king but the Portuguese threw him in jail. Before Nzinga, women were not allowed to rule in her kingdom but, after her brother died, she took over as queen. Queen Nzinga would not let the Portuguese stay in power and take advantage of her people. The leaders of other countries were unhappy with a female leader and tried to remove Nzinga from the throne but she ruled well! She offered a safe place to runaway slaves.

Nzinga started a war to defeat the Portuguese which lasted 30 years. This fight eventually led Angola to their independence in 1975. She was the first African leader to create a treaty with European leaders. According to legends, during the treaty meeting, the Portuguese governor arranged a floor mat for her to sit, while he sat on a chair above her. This was a sign of disrespect which Nzinga did not allow. She ordered a servant to lie down on the ground on hands and knees and then sat on the back of the servant to proceed with the meeting.

Queen Nzinga was an outstanding woman who was **cunning**, strong and never allowed disrespect nor injustice.

HANNIBAL
OF CARTHAGE

In 247 BC, one of the greatest military leaders in history was born to the Carthage empire! He was the son of an army general and his name was Hannibal Barca. Growing up, Hannibal wanted to be just like his father.

Hannibal had an army of 100,000 men and many elephants. He was feared by the Romans and was their strongest enemy. Hannibal is celebrated in history for bringing his men across the great Alps mountain range to invade Northern Italy. The army faced tough weather conditions and the mountain **trek** was difficult. By the time they got to the other side, there were only 26,000 men remaining and very few elephants. Still, Hannibal led them bravely into battle against the Romans. He led his men to win many battles!

Hannibal was such a great **strategist** that his **military tactics** are still studied and adopted today. Even his greatest enemies copied his military ideas. He is listed as one of the greatest military commanders in history.

RANAVALONA I

"I will worship no god but those of my ancestors!" said Ranavalona, the **benevolent** queen of Madagascar. She was born a commoner and her father worked for the king. When she was a young girl, her father warned the king of a plan to take his life and to thank him, the king adopted Ranavalona as his own daughter. She eventually married the king's son and became Madagascar's queen. Ranavalona did not have any children so when the king died, her nephew was next in line to be king. She knew her nephew would try to kill her but, luckily, she was able to outsmart him.

During her 33 year **reign**, she promoted **self-reliance** in Madagascar, cutting ties with France and Britain. She outlawed practicing Christianity in Madagascar, so that the people would respect their ancient beliefs and practices. Ranavalona thanked the French and the English for the good they had done but did not want them to change the **customs** of her people's ancestors. Due to her great strength and leadership, neither France nor Britain were able to take control of the country.

She is known and celebrated today for maintaining Madagascar's cultural **heritage** and defending her country against powerful European nations, in a time when most of the African continent was under European rule.

SHAKA ZULU

Long ago, there lived a very powerful man! His name was Shaka - King of the Zulu people. King Shaka grew up with his mother and loved her very much. When he was a young boy, the children in his clan were very mean to him. So, Shaka spent his time taking care of sheep and cattle. He showed great bravery in protecting the animals. He even fought a leopard and killed it with his bare hands!

When King Shaka was 21, he became a soldier. He was very good at protection and **defence** which he learnt as a young shepherd. King Shaka was a strong leader and an even stronger warrior. With King Shaka as chief, the Zulu army was a large, mighty tribe of more than 20,000 men! He taught them how to make weapons and shields and showed them the best way to protect their families. The Zulu tribe defeated every nation that tried to rule them.

King Shaka was very just and fair. He taught his people to share **resources** equally, work hard, and respect the elderly. King Shaka was one of the greatest leaders of the Zulu people.

GLOSSARY:
Do you know these words?

Pharaoh *(n)* -   A ruler in ancient Egypt.

Treaty *(n)* -   A formal agreement between countries or states.

Monument *(n)* -   A statue, building, or other structure built to celebrate an important person or event.

Emperor *(n)* -   A sovereign ruler of an empire.

Empire *(n)* -   An extensive group of states or countries ruled over by a single ruler.

Revered *(adj.)* -   Deeply respected and admired.

Synagogue *(n)* -   A building in which Jews meet for religious worship or instruction.

Mosque *(n)* -   A Muslim place of worship.

Wealthy *(adj.)* -   Rich.

Pilgrimage *(n)* -   A journey to a place of particular interest or significance.

Generosity *(n)* -   The quality of being kind and generous.

Umbilical cord *(n)* -   A flexible cordlike structure that attaches a human to their mother during pregnancy.

Slave *(n)* -   A person who is the legal property of another and is forced to obey them.

Cunning *(adj.)* -	Showing skill in achieving one's ends by deceit or clever actions.
Trek *(n)* -	A long journey, especially one made on foot.
Strategist *(n)* -	A person skilled in planning action or policy, especially in war or politics.
Military tactic *(n)* -	An action or strategy carefully planned by the armed forces of a country to achieve a particular goal.
Benevolent *(adj.)* -	Well meaning and kind.
Reign *(n)* -	The period of holding royal office.
Self-reliance *(n)* -	Reliance on one's own powers and resources rather than those of others.
Outlaw *(v)* -	Ban or make illegal.
Custom *(n)* -	A traditional and widely accepted way of behaving or doing something that is specific to a particular society, place, or time.
Heritage *(n)* -	Valued objects and qualities such as historic buildings and cultural traditions that have been passed down from previous generations.
Defence *(n)* -	A means of protecting something from attack.
Resource *(n)* -	A stock or supply of money, materials, staff, and other things a person or country owns

Definitions were adapted from the **Oxford English Dictionary
and are in order of appearance in each story.*

Lightning Source UK Ltd.
Milton Keynes UK
UKHW051241281019
352441UK00006B/53/P